D-DAY

Plus Fifty Years

THE NORMANDY BEACHES REVISITED

TEXT AND PHOTOGRAPHY BY HENRY RASMUSSEN

TOP TEN PUBLISHING

First published in 1994 by Top Ten Publishing Corporation, 42 Digital Drive #5, Novato, California 94949, U.S.A.

© Top Ten Publishing Corporation

Printed and bound in Hong Kong.

ISBN 1-879301-06-7

All color photography was executed by the author. Kodak film and Mamiya cameras were employed exclusively. The historic photos were supplied by the Bundesarchiv, Koblenz, the Imperial War Museum, London, the National Archives, Washington D.C. In Normandy, the author received useful assistance from Arlette Gondré, Marc Jacquinot, Philippe Jutras, Mari Laurent, Chauvin Pierre. For their help with editing and proofreading, the author is indebted to David Gardella, Kathryn Johns, Nancy Kivette, Jay Lamm. Finally, the author extends special thanks to Tom Toldrian, without whose support the book could not have been done.

THE BIRTH OF BATTLEFIELD NOSTALGIA

I was born in Copenhagen on the day Hitler attacked Poland. After the Nazis blitzed their way across Denmark and Norway, my father was sent to Germany, a forced laborer. Mother and I had to go to Norway to stay with her parents.

Our town lay in a fjord. It was a harbor, held by a strong German garrison. Watching the war, its ships and soldiers, vehicles, weapons—the scarlet sky after bomb raids—became an obsession.

Food and clothing were scarce during these years, but I never knew it. It was the best time of my life. I was old enough to be taken in by the illusion, but too young to truly understand.

After the war, us kids played in the abandoned trenches. Helmets and other memorabilia were to be found everywhere. This was the birth of a battlefield nostalgia that refused to go away.

The fiftieth anniversary of D-Day gave me an opportunity to relive my childhood. This was *my* motive for visiting Normandy—*the* battlefield of battlefields. For someone who fought there, the reasons to go back would certainly be different.

Yet, when all is seen and relived we submit to the same reality: War is absurd, and mankind must strive to create no more battlefields.

Henry Rasmussen, San Rafael, January 1994.

CONTENTS

VESTIGES OF WAR

The gray, blustery morning of June 6, 1944, witnessed the mightiest invasion armada ever assembled. Five thousand ships and two thousand planes transported one hundred sixty thousand men to a rendezvous with destiny. Three thousand gave their lives for a foothold strong enough to overwhelm the enemy—it was the beginning of the end. Now, fifty years have passed, and time has healed the wounds. But not all scars have disappeared. Not every vestige vanished. Images of the distant war still linger in such secret places as shallow tide pools and shady country lanes.

CONCRETE
ABSTRACTION

· · · · · · · · · · · · · · · ·

*Once indestructible, a
German gun emplacement
at Grandcamp is slowly
being devoured by the sea.
The crumbling colossus,
stark, grotesque, stands as
a macabre memento of
a turbulent past.*

RIPPLES OF REMEMBRANCE

*Wind and water create
pleasing patterns at Omaha—
Bloody Omaha—covering
the tracks of tragedy.
Despite nature's oblivion,
thoughts of the legion of lives
lost in this scenic
setting is never far from
a visitor's mind.*

A DREAM BLOWN
TO OBLIVION

A fisherman with means and dreams, so the legend says, built his home on the cliff overlooking Omaha Beach. Still unfinished, the Germans used it as an observation post. Shelling blew it to pieces.

DRAMA AT DAWN

*Imagine the scene that
morning. Men rising from the
surf. Gray silhouettes of
warships looming offshore.
And, suddenly, from one
of their cannons, the flash of
a blast. Then the flight,
the howling, the thunderous
impact of the shell that
shattered the wall.*

FORGOTTEN FACADE

Norman resolve has swept away most traces of war. Only on rare occasions will a searching eye find a forgotten facade such as this, its pockmarked stucco recalling house-to-house combat in Sainte-Mère-Église.

NEW SCARS
ON AN OLD WALL

A thirteenth century wall at
Abbey Ardenne, where
Canada's North Novas fought
fanatical Hitler Youths in
bloody battles, displays scars
from half a century ago
as casually as a decorative
layer of patina.

LONG-DISTANCE DUELERS

On D-Day, four 150-mm cannons at Longues lost a duel with half a dozen invasion force cruisers, but only after having chased away the command ship of British 3d Infantry. One of the cannons (left) was still intact when the crew surrendered. A 50-mm cannon (below) points its barrel at the port of Courseulles.

HOLE IN ONE

• • • • • • • • • • • • • • • • •

*Gunner Jack Boardman
shot a Sherman shell right
through the aperture of
a bunker in Omaha Beach's
Strongpoint 62.*

SAVED FROM
THE SEA

· · · · · · · · · · · · · · · ·

*Of 32 amphibious tanks
launched off Omaha
Beach on D-Day morning,
27 foundered in rough
seas, many sinking with the
crew trapped inside. After
nearly four decades on the
ocean floor, two of the
33-ton hulks were salvaged
by Jacques Lemonchois,
a local diver and
scrap-iron merchant.*

SIMPLE STEN GUN

· · · · · · · · · · · · · · ·

It was basic in design and cheap to make, but the main submachine gun of the British jammed easily and was accurate only at close range. This rusty example was extracted from the muddy bottom of the Courseulles Canal.

SOPHISTICATED SCHMEISSER

· · · · · · · · · · · · · · · · ·

*The principal German
submachine gun comfortably
outperformed its Allied
counterparts, with a firing
speed that spread fear.
Albeit superb in design and
finish, it was also too
costly to produce.*

CAUSE & EFFECT

● ● ● ● ● ● ● ● ● ● ● ● ●

An American hand grenade (above) shows its malign appearance among innocent flowers on Utah Beach. The German jacket (opposite) was discovered in a bunker at Omaha Beach.

**TREASURE
HUNTER'S TREAT**

· · · · · · · · · · · · · ·

*This Colt 45 was uncovered
in the early eighties by
André Bonne, avid collector
of D-Day memorabilia,
while exploring the rotting
wreckage of a landing
barge on Utah Beach with
a metal detector.*

HELMET
OF AN UNKNOWN
SOLDIER

*This British helmet, its
D-Day marking (the white
band) still intact, was
photographed on a stretch
of Sword Beach where
more than two hundred men
died during the first few
minutes of battle.*

LEFT BEHIND

· ·

*An American helmet
(left) washed up among the
pebbles covering portions
of Omaha Beach. A German
helmet (above) abandoned
in the desolate dunes
of Utah Beach.*

SIGN OF RECOGNITION

A hedge-lined lane
leading out of Mont Fleury
was the route taken by
British 50th Infantry on its
way to free Bayeux half
a century ago. A sign
commemorates the Road
of Liberation.

exploiting the window of opportunity available to them during the first few days of June—a period when moon and tide favored amphibious operations. Another opportunity would not present itself until later in the month.

The storm had reached hurricane force in the Channel during the night, prompting the Kriegsmarine to keep its ships in harbor, the Luftwaffe its craft on the ground. Surely, Rommel reasoned, the Allies would have taken similar action.

Rommel leaned back in the seat of his car and gave Corporal Daniel, the chauffeur, a nod. The big Horch eased off, crushing torn branches as it rolled down the avenue. The time was seven in the morning. The date, June 5. The destination, Berchtesgaden, Hitler's command center. The task, to change the Führer's mind about troop deployment in the West. But first on the itinerary, a stop at the Rommel residence in Herrlingen, where his wife expected him that same evening. The next day, June 6, was her birthday.

After the spectacular blitzkrieg successes of 1939 and 1940, by spring of 1944 Hitler's fortunes had taken a turn for the worse. The Russians were smashing his armies in the East. Half a million men had been lost during the

GENERALS' DISAGREEMENT

· · · · · · · · · · · · · · · · · · · ·

Hitler allowed his generals to quarrel. Pictured right, commanders of Army Group West (left to right): General Geyr von Schweppenburg, Panzer Group West; General Johannes Blaskowitz, Army Group G; Marshal Hugo Sperrle, 3d Air Fleet; Field Marshal Gerd von Rundstedt, Supreme Commander; Field Marshal Erwin Rommel, Army Group B; Admiral Theodor Krancke, Naval Group West. Above: No friendly faces when von Rundstedt and Rommel posed for the photographer.

DETERMINED TEAM

• •

Eisenhower forged unity among his commanders.
Above: Getting ready for a group shot, (left to
right) General Omar Bradley, 1st U.S. Army; Admiral
Bertram Ramsey, Royal Navy; Marshal Trafford
Leigh-Mallory, Royal Air Force; General Walter
Bedell-Smith, Chief of Staff; Marshal Arthur Tedder,
Deputy Supreme Commander; General Dwight
Eisenhower, Supreme Commander; General Bernard
Montgomery, 21st Army Group, commander
of all land forces on D-Day.

Below: Forced laborers build a gun emplacement on the Atlantic Wall. Bottom: A finished bunker. Waiting for the invasion was hard on morale. Rommel, constantly inspecting troops for readiness, rewarded good performance with accordions.

disastrous winter campaign. On the home front, Allied bombers were pounding citizen morale as well as manufacturing capacity to a pulp.

The fact that an invasion by the Allies would establish a second front, thus forcing a further dilution of Germany's rapidly thinning resources, did not worry Hitler. He welcomed it. True to his fatalistic nature he believed that the upcoming battle would give him an opportunity to finish off the British once and for all—confining them to the isolation of their island for good.

T he key element in his strategy was the Atlantic Wall, a more or less continuous chain of fortifications stretching from the north of Norway to the south of France. The problem was, as Hitler's generals knew full well, with the losses in the East, a lack of first rate troops made effective defense of the long front impossible. Difficult choices had to be made regarding the most likely invasion targets, and the limited assets arranged accordingly.

The Germans faced yet another problem—a serious disagreement within the High Command concerning basic strategy. Field Marshal Gerd von Rundstedt, the crusty veteran chosen by Hitler for the post of Supreme Commander West, held

THE GUNS OF LINDEMANN

• •

Some of the biggest guns ever built formed
formidable strongpoints along Hitler's Atlantic Wall.
Above: This 16-inch-caliber monster, one of
three such guns in Batterie Lindemann near Calais,
sent a 2,260-pound projectile on a twenty-six mile
flight. The barrel alone measured nearly
sixty-one feet and weighed almost 50,000 pounds.
Left: An early-warning system employed
radar. This is the Würzburg type.

ASSEMBLING AN ALLIED ARSENAL

. . . .

Every pasture and waterway in southern England become a depot. Below: Shermans crowd a field. Bottom: Landing craft line a pier as far as the eye can see. Opposite top: Bombs for Flying Fortresses mingle with sheep in a farmer's field.

the conventional view, which called for the defending army to be positioned well inland. Here it would engage the invaders in grand scale battles. Generals would move their divisions like pawns on a chessboard, attacking, retreating, entrapping, encircling—all in accordance with the rules of textbook warfare.

Rommel, still the maverick, thought otherwise. The invaders had to be charged on the beaches, he argued—at the moment when they were most vulnerable. The attackers must be thrown back before they could gain foothold. According to this strategy the defenders should be located very close to the coast, where they could be deployed both quickly and accurately.

Hitler, trusting no one, and having therefore reserved the final decision for himself, had settled on a compromise, crippling both plans.

Thus it was on D-Day Minus One, June 5, out of the most formidable formations in Normandy, the SS Panzer Divisions, that the 21st Panzer—the closest division to a likely invasion beach—was positioned south of Caen, twenty miles away. Another division, Panzer Lehr, was kept near Le Mans. It would take this unit one entire day to reach the coast.

THUNDERBOLTS TO SECURE THE SKY

● ●

Allied supremacy in the air was to be ensured
by an armada of 15,000 airplanes. Of these, 4,000 were
fighter bombers, like the partially assembled
Thunderbolts in the scene below, showing a Liberty ship
relinquishing its cargo in a British port.

PRE·D·DAY DESTRUCTION

• •

Over 70,000 tons of bombs rained destruction on enemy communications. Below: Rail bridges in the bomb sight. Bottom: Occupation forces lived in fear of the menace from the sky. Opposite: A Halifax over German installations in Pas de Calais.

The units manning the string of strongpoints along the coast were all stationary, staffed by convalescents from the Russian front, over-aged conscripts and forced laborers.

Enveloped in the normally calming comfort of the Horch, Rommel wrestled with the realities of his dilemma, finding no rest. The drumming sound of rain beating down on the convertible top, and the mad hammering of mud and stones on the wheel wells, added to his tension. He was resigned to the fact that nothing could be done to strengthen the defenses beyond the mining program, the obstacle planting, and the building projects. The stationary units were also firmly established. The panzer divisions, however, *their* deployment *must* be changed.

On the British side of the Channel—only a few hours before Rommel set out on his journey—a group of men were gathered in the oak paneled library at Southwick House, a posh mansion near Portsmouth accommodating the Overlord nerve center. General Eisenhower, one of the men seated in a circle of easy chairs, played with the lucky coins he had carried in his pocket since the African campaign. His subliminal

preoccupation made a tiny metallic clink that was drowned out by the ominous urgency of the howling wind and spattering rain.

The men sat in silence while the Supreme Commander shifted his gaze from face to face. They all reflected the tension of the moment. His own expression was calm, collected when he finally spoke to confirm that the decision to go ahead with the invasion stood firm.

General Dwight Eisenhower was not a battlefield hero. As a matter of fact he had never tasted the fear of front line fighting. He was a desk soldier. Yet, he proved to be the perfect choice for Supreme Commander. His military training had been extensive: the mandatory West Point initiation, the priming of talent under General MacArthur, the coming of age as head of Washington's War Plans Division, the baptism as leader of men when charged with overall command of the North African and Sicilian landings. All of this, in addition to his personality, gave him the edge. At once both friendly and firm, tolerant and tenacious, he was able to forge cohesion from a congestion of views, a divergence of egos. He became the great coordinator, the grand conciliator.

MONSTROUS FIGHTING MACHINE

• •

Advanced weapons favored the Germans. The Schmeisser (opposite bottom), the Panzerwerfer (opposite top), the Königstiger (above), the Nebelwerfer (left)—known and feared in France as Moaning Minnie— were all superior to Allied counterparts.

A hostile environment awaited the invaders. Below: The dreaded "hedgehogs," metal tetrahedras placed fifteen feet apart, and often mined. Bottom: Sentry atop a concrete seawall obstacle. Opposite bottom: Barbed wire protects the perimeter of a strongpoint.

Mending fences, especially when dealing with men of such strong convictions as Montgomery and Patton, was not an easy task. In his new role as commander of the land forces, Montgomery—the hero of El Alamein—could be kept in line only with difficulty. And Patton, the bold-spirited warrior with the hot head and the sharp tongue, was outraged when placed in charge of an army that, for the benefit of deceiving the Germans, existed only in the realm of spy masters.

Originally, D-Day had been set for June 5. However, to enable all units of the vast fleet to converge at the predetermined time and place, the convoys with the farthest distance to travel had set sail well ahead of that date. On June 1, Allied weather forecasters became aware of a series of depressions forming over the North Atlantic—the same systems also observed by German meteorologists.

On the morning of June 4, with low clouds, high seas and driving rain in the weather report, General Eisenhower decided to postpone the invasion for twenty-four hours. Every convoy, wherever its position, had to be given the turn-around code—a logistical nightmare since strict radio silence had been imposed.

A DAY AT THE BEACH

• •

*After assuming responsibility for the defense
of the Atlantic coast, Rommel applied his cunning genius
to devising a variety of beach obstacles, one
of the most destructive being the "Hemmbalken", wooden
contraptions fitted with mines and metal blades
designed to cut open the bottoms of landing craft. The
photograph above, taken shortly before the
invasion, shows Rommel (third from left) inspecting
his handiwork on a Normandy beach .*

After their long wait, the troops are eager to go.
Below: A military convoy crowds a city street. Bottom:
American Marines board their LCVP (Landing
Craft Vehicle Personnel). Opposite: Shermans rumble
onto the deck of an LCT (Landing Craft Tank).

In one instance a convoy of 140 ships could not be located. It took until late in the day before a lone Walrus aircraft spotted the fleet below a blanket of low clouds. Dropping a message container right on the deck of the commodore's vessel, the pilot circled the convoy until he could confirm that a new course had been charted. Disaster was averted at the last moment.

T he road that led to Overlord was long and hard, tracing its origin to a cross-Channel invasion plan found in proposals authored by Albert Wedemeyer, a lieutenant-colonel in the War Plans Division.

His strategy was dictated by a true grasp of the German Army and its tactical thinking, ironically acquired at the source—the *Kriegsakademie*—where he was a student as late as 1938.

The cross-Channel invasion plan, code named Roundup, became a cornerstone of the Marshall Memorandum—authored by Eisenhower and presented to Churchill early in 1942.

Set for the spring of 1943, the invasion was put off again and again, mainly due to a British wait-and-see attitude. Mindful of the efficiency of the German fighting machine, and keen on keeping his irreplaceable resources, Churchill managed to

The Allied air force comprised more than 4,000 bombers—the Luftwaffe could muster less than 200 in France. Opposite: A Mitchell passes part of the invasion fleet. Nearly 12,000 tons of bombs awaited defenders of the Atlantic Wall.

divert American readiness into less dangerous, peripheral actions, such as Operation Torch, the invasion of French North Africa.

Operation Overlord, with its thrust into the heart of Europe, had other detractors as well, in particular American commanders in the Pacific. But Midway changed everything—the outcome in Asia was now no longer in doubt. By spring of 1944, with the Russians desperately needing a second front to weaken German resistance in the East, Overlord could wait no longer.

E isenhower's arrival in London in January 1944, finally catalyzed the organization responsible for Overlord planning into a thoroughly homogeneous—although not always completely harmonious—team.

The choice of Normandy had already been made. This coast, although further away than Pas de Calais, was less heavily defended, but still met the distance requirement—determined by the operational limit of a Spitfire fighter plane.

The buildup was soon in full swing. Convoy after convoy of transatlantic ships emptied their bellies in British ports. The idyllic countryside began filling with war materiel—everything from tanks to trucks, airplanes to ammunition.

UNCHALLENGED IN THE CHANNEL

. . . .

While the German Navy kept its ships in harbor—forced
to safety by hurricane winds—an Allied armada
of 7,000 ships took advantage of a break in the weather
that had eluded German forecasters. Opposite
top: One of 221 destroyers in the force. Far left: A convoy
of LCTs. Left: One of two midget subs used
to guide the fleet to the target.

Opposite: Night of June 5. Four commandos from 22nd Independent Parachute Company, British 6th Airborne, synchronize their watches. Below: Paras board for the cross-Channel flight. Bottom: A Horsa glider takes off, towed by a bomber.

Tent camps sprouted all across England, and the jagged coastline saw an accumulation of strange ships, some of them dummies—there to deceive the few Luftwaffe planes purposely let through the wall of fighter protection.

The wheels of this immense machinery were already spinning when the sudden postponement stopped them in their tracks. To the Allies, the storm seemed to be a disaster. To the Germans, it seemed to be a break. But what the Allied weather experts discovered, and their German counterparts did not, was a one-day lull in the storm. This was the great chance provided, as it seemed, by providence. And Eisenhower took it, issuing his on-again order on the morning of June 5. The Day of Decision had arrived.

The moon still hung bright in the night sky as two British midget subs surfaced a few miles off the Normandy coast and began sending homing signals to the armada chugging through the rough waters of the Channel.

At about the same time, Hitler, holed up in his Obersalzberg holiday house, prepared to go to bed. Heavily sedated, he was soon asleep.

The Führer had issued strict orders not to wake him until ten o'clock the following morning.

Acrashing sound jolted the two German sentries at the Caen Canal Bridge out of their nocturnal trance. Seconds later, they were stunned by the sight of commandos dashing toward them. The next moment, one of the sentries lay dead. The other ran for his life. The time was twenty minutes past midnight. A crack unit from British 6th Airborne, whose symbol was the winged Pegasus, had just crash-landed its gliders next to the bridge, initiating the first D-Day ground action. Pegasus Bridge became a monument to these men, whose daring mission was a key to Allied success.

PEGASUS BRIDGE

ANATOMY OF A MIDNIGHT ASSAULT

ON THE NIGHT of June 5, four minutes before eleven, six Halifax bombers took off from Tarrant Rushton airfield, Dorset, England. In tow were six Horsa gliders, each carrying thirty commandos from 6th Airborne Division. A scene on the opposite page (bottom right) shows aircraft forming up for takeoff. Pictured in the photo to the right are Horsas and Halifaxes under way to France. **THE TARGETS,** two vital bridges—one crossing the Caen Canal, the other spanning the Orne River—wait unsuspecting in the moonlight. Opposite top, a view of the canal bridge—Pegasus Bridge—five decades later. **THE LANDING SITE,** a marshy meadow adjacent to the canal bridge, is pictured (bottom right) as it looks today. **COMMANDER** of 6th Airborne was General Richard "Windy" Gale. On opposite page (bottom left), the general briefs his troops on the eve of action. Camouflage cream, mixed with burnt cork, was used to darken the faces.

BADGE OF THE BRAVE

A vital D-Day objective was to seize and hold the eastern flank, a task given the men of 6th Airborne—who wore the Pegasus emblem. Although the mission was their baptism of fire, it was executed with dash and bravery, giving fame and glory to the winged symbol.

INCREDIBLE FEAT OF FLYING

SEVEN MINUTES past midnight—it was now the morning of D-Day—the gliders cast off from their tow planes. A series of dives and turns, executed according to a carefully calculated timetable (relying only on compasses and stop watches), brought the gliders from seven thousand feet to five hundred. Sixteen minutes past midnight the lead glider crash-landed on the ground and came to rest a short distance from the bridge. The aerial photo depicts the canal bridge and the three gliders in the meadow.

MOMENTS LATER, the assault was in full swing. To the right, the bridge from the vantage point of the attacking commandos. On the left was a German antitank gun, on the right a pillbox. **ONE COMMANDO WAS KILLED,** cut down by machine gun fire while traversing the span shown in the color picture opposite.

TWO OF THE THREE GLIDERS are seen in the photograph at the top of the opposite page, two days after the bridge was captured.

EYEWITNESS TO AN HISTORIC EVENT

IN A SMALL CAFÉ beside the canal bridge, proprietors Georges Gondrée and his wife Thérèsa—asleep in the upstairs bedroom—were awakened by the jarring crashes caused by the rough-landing gliders. The photograph to the right shows the view from the Gondrée's bedroom. **WHEN THE SHOOTING BEGAN,** they fetched their daughters, six-year-old Georgette and infant Arlette, and hid with them in the cellar. **THROUGH A WINDOW** (bottom right), Georges watched events unfold. He realized the bridge was under attack, and when English-speaking soldiers knocked on the door, he welcomed them with open arms.

THE GONDRÉE CAFÉ was the first building, and the Gondrées were the first French, to be liberated—a fact they never forgot. The Gondrées turned the café into a shrine to the men who fought so gallantly for freedom. Opposite page, the café as it looks today—still a gathering place for veterans and friends of 6th Airborne.

GIFT OF THE GONDREES

Unbeknown to the Germans, Thérèsa understood their language and passed to the Resistance valuable information she picked up from bridge defenders patronizing the café. After the war, she became the beloved host to returning veterans, running the café until her death in 1984. Today, daughter Arlette keeps the flame alive.

COUP DE MAIN COMMEMORATED

ORDERS FOR THE ATTACK on the Pegasus Bridge used the French phrase *coup de main* to describe the daredevil nature of the operation. Images on these pages illustrate close brushes with death experienced by the fearless men of D Company. The photograph to the right shows glider number three after landing. The force of the impact shot pilot and crew right through the fuselage. Survival was miraculous. Moments later they gathered their scattered weapons and attacked. **ANOTHER BRUSH WITH DEATH** was experienced by Major John Howard, force commander, whose helmet—preserved in a commemorative museum next to the Gondrée Café, and pictured in the photo opposite—was pierced by a bullet that grazed his skull.

A GLIDER PILOT'S BERET (right), with its special badge, is also among the mementos displayed in the museum. **BRITISH TROOPS** cross the the Pegasus Bridge in the photograph opposite (top), three days after liberation.

HOMAGE TO FALLEN HEROES

SOLE CASUALTY of the landing at Pegasus Bridge was Corporal Knox, who was thrown out of the glider at impact and drowned in a pond. For Knox, the mission was over before it began, but his memory is kept alive. The photograph at the top of the page shows a small cross, placed at the foot of his grave marker in a Bénouville cemetery on June 6, 1992. **HIS RUSTY GUN,** a Bren, was discovered in the muddy pond four decades later, and is returned to the site in the photo opposite. **THE MIDNIGHT ASSAULT** on Pegasus Bridge was a prelude to large-scale operations by British paratroopers. Many died in planes shot down by German flak. The photo opposite (bottom left) is a poignant commentary. **LUFTWAFFE ACTION** was spotty. Opposite (bottom right), a Messerschmidt in hiding. **MANY PARAS WERE KILLED** or wounded as they hit the ground. A recently found photo (right), snapped by a Wehrmacht correspondent, shows Germans tending to British paras.

DROPPING DEAD, DIGGING IN

THE FIRST WAVE of airborne troops jumped from low-flying DC-3s at 0050. Due to heavy flak and high winds, many landed far away from their assigned drop zones. Some even fell behind enemy lines—with tragic results, as evidenced by the photograph to the right, found in a German archive. **LATER WAVES** of airborne troops, now arriving by glider, also experienced heavy casualties. Of sixty-eight units scheduled to arrive at 0320, fifty made it to the landing zone. The others broke their tow lines, were shot down, or lost their bearings. The photos on opposite page show elements of 6th Airborne entrenched in apple orchards on the outskirts of Ranville, east of Pegasus Bridge.

THE PARACHUTE WINGS, right—attached to a smock in the Pegasus Museum—were awarded after seven jumps. **BINOCULARS** (opposite), were a vital part of the load carried by a paratrooper. This action-worn pair was manufactured by Taylor+Hobson in 1941.

DEATH OF A SNIPER

THE VILLAGE of Bénouville, just up the road from Pegasus Bridge, was the site of fierce fighting on D-Day. Occupied by a small German force (1st Panzer Engineering Company, 716th Infantry Division), the village was attacked by British paras (A Company, 7th Parachute Battalion) commanded by Major Nigel Taylor.

HOUSE-TO-HOUSE COMBAT reduced Taylor's force to thirty men by midday, when help arrived in the form of Lord Lovat's commandos (No. 6 Commando, Special Service Brigade).

SMALL ARMS FIRE failed to dislodge a sniper barricaded in the church tower, until a well-placed grenade blew a hole in the belfry, killing the dogged defender. The black and white photos show the fallen German and a horse-drawn cart brought up to take away his body.

THE TOWER was repaired after the war. The color photos show the church as it appears today, with one of its walls left intact, still displaying the mementos of a distant drama.

68

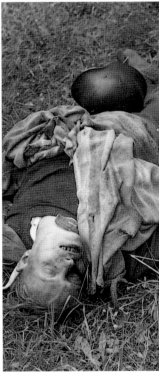

MISSPENT VALOR AT MERVILLE

THE ATTACK on *Batterie Merville* rivaled that on Pegasus Bridge in daring and execution. The pre-D-Day aerial view shows the effect of unsuccessful bomb raids. One of the bunkers took a hit, but its six-foot thick concrete remained intact. It was now up to the commandos.

THE STRONGPOINT, located near the beach town of Franceville—about six miles due west of Pegasus Bridge—threatened D-Day landings at Sword Beach with what was thought to be four 150-mm guns. On the opposite page, a scene illustrating life inside the concrete bunkers.

BRITISH COMMANDOS attacked at 0430 on D-Day morning. Hand-to-hand combat left 65 dead and wounded. But the feared guns were found to be of 75-mm caliber—their 13-pound projectiles would have had little disruptive effect.

TODAY, only cattle (their hoof prints pit the sand in the photo near right) seek shelter in the empty bunkers, and where gun barrels once protruded (opposite), now empty holes gape.

Decision Day was less than two hours old, when fifteen thousand paras from 82d All American and 101st Screaming Eagles began dropping from low-flying Dakotas all across the Contentin Peninsula. Mission: securing the western flank. The town of Sainte-Mère-Église saw one parachutist land right on its church steeple. Unable to cut himself loose, he avoided being killed by acting dead, all while the battle raged in the square below. To this day, with a life-size paratrooper in perennial suspension from the steeple, the town still pays homage to its liberating heroes.

PARATROOPS LOST IN PARADISE

IT TOOK NO LESS THAN 822 DC-3s to carry the American airborne troops to the their six drop zones. Suddenly, peaceful pastures were buzzing with activity—to the consternation of the cows, as stolid then as today (near right).

GLIDERS FOLLOWED carrying more men as well as heavy supplies. A Waco (this page, bottom) lies intact after the mission (note the ever-present cows). The Waco—designed by Waco Aircraft, Troy, Ohio—featured a fuselage of wood and steel, covered with plywood and fabric.

NOT SO FORTUNATE was this British-built Horsa glider (opposite bottom), broken apart by the force of a violent landing. A limp parachute hangs from a tree like a flag flown in mourning.

LOST AND LONELY, the men groped in the dark, not knowing if the next man was friend or foe. Incidentally, some of the Germans they faced were also airborne, relegated to infantry duty for lack of aircraft—seen opposite (top), a *Fallshirmsjäger* with the rare FG-42 rifle.

FIRST TOWN TO BE LIBERATED

SAINTE-MÈRE-ÉGLISE, on the main road between Paris and Cherbourg, lay squarely in the middle of the American drop zone. It was the first town to be liberated when men from the 505th Parachute Infantry, 82d Airborne, were dropped from 600 feet, right into the square.

THE ANCIENT CHURCH (this page, top) was a German holdout, with snipers and artillery spotters barricading themselves inside. In the photo opposite (top), the attack begins. It is hard to imagine that such a peaceful setting was once the scene of so much violence—the doors remain as mute witnesses (opposite bottom).

GERMAN ARTILLERY SHELLED the town in a desperate attempt to recapture it, but the Americans held on. Pictured to the right (bottom), destruction in one of the main road crossings. The color photo (right center) shows the same location today. Twenty-two civilians were innocent victims of the fierce fighting—one man buried his infant daughter in the arms of his wife.

STUCK ON THE STEEPLE

Dropping from 600 feet, it took less than forty seconds for the parachutist to hit the ground—not much time in which to correct one's direction of descent. One jumper got stuck on the steeple, an incident made famous in the movie "The Longest Day," and remembered ever since in the form of a dummy suspended from the bell tower.

GUNS IN THE HOUSE OF GOD

MACHINE-GUN BULLETS were flying in the sanctuary when men from the 82d Airborne dislodged the Germans hiding inside. Scars from the battle are visible to this day—fragments of the graceful old arches, shot away by the bullets, are still missing, as seen on this page (bottom), and on the opposite page (far right).

THE OLD STAINED-GLASS WINDOWS were completely destroyed in the fierce fighting. The new windows of the church—whose most ancient sections date back to the Eleventh Century—proudly memorialize the town's pivotal role during the early stages of the invasion. Troopers and chutes figure frequently in the designs. One of the windows was unveiled in 1969—on the 25th Anniversary—and was funded in part by donations from veterans of the 505th Parachute Regiment—the town's liberators.

THE POIGNANCY of the war-time memories is reflected in participants' faces during a 1946 memorial service in the church (right top).

SURVIVING STORE

The observer with an eye for details will notice the front of the E. Castel clothing store in many wartime photos. Should the observer pay a visit to Sainte-Mère-Église today, he would find that the front has not changed. Incredibly, the proprietor is also still the same—able to tell the visitor that the large windows were smashed by flying debris. That was the only damage.

A PLACE FOR REVELS AND REMEMBRANCE

THE AMERICANS WERE HEROES, and treated as such. Dressed in exotic but utilitarian uniforms, replete with bulging pockets—not to forget the paratrooper knife strapped to the leg—they looked the part in a no-nonsense way. And they were also chivalrous—the return home after terrifying days and nights in makeshift shelters was a happy occasion, especially with the help of a GI (right center). In other settings the elation of liberation took other forms—the townspeople opened their homes to the heroes, and let the *calvados* flow (bottom right).

THE STUDENT OF WAR NOSTALGIA finds Sainte-Mère-Église filled with mementos and memorable places, such as a bar whose name recalls the date of liberation (this page top), a pump in the square which the paratroopers used to wash off the dust of battle as well as to quench their thirst (bottom far right), and the picturesque well from which the war-time mayor rescued a drowning parachutist (opposite).

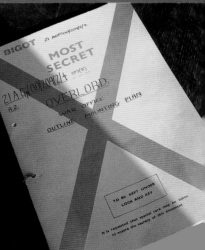

SCREAMING EAGLES STRIKE

THE DOZEN HOUSES that surround the Sainte-Marie-du-Mont church, its distinctive tower visible for miles (right top), still stand as they did fifty years ago when they witnessed the first probing actions of the Screaming Eagles.

SCATTERED LIKE CONFETTI across the fields, the men were separated from comrades and commanders. But slowly small groups gathered. In the pre-dawn darkness the villagers saw from behind shuttered windows a lone paratrooper hide in the corner behind a pump in the square. From here he calmly picked off one German after the other, clearing the way for the attack. The photo to the right (center) captures the scene around the pump after liberation. Opposite page, another angle of the street corner. The color photo (right bottom) shows the same spot today.

OVER THE YEARS returning veterans have scribbled their names across the photograph opposite (top), on display in a memorabilia shop housed in a building next to the pump.

Leon Smiles
79 Div 304 Med.
2097 S.W. 13 Terr
Boynton Beach Fla.
33426

7/ Bryant 7/4/48

Sgt. J. T. Rogan
1944 + 1988

Bob Snow
101st End Co.N
WS 6/1/44
6/1/88

Roger Reimon
Davenport Iowa
XXX Recon

Howard Manorie
A Co 505 Para Regt T.

James W. Glenn
C Co 502 PIR 101 AB
Ste Mère Église France
June 44

Hugh O. Roberts 23/6/88
6/6/44 2nd Bn 502 Para. Inf
Bethlehem, Pa
"Mont Fleur" (début)
Grenville Eaton. Pilot/Pathfinder.
4am. 6.6.44. Shoreham By Sea.
Sussex G.B.

S/Sgt Kent D. White
92nd Bomb Group
8th Air Force S.L.C. Utah

Denis M. Persons
"G" 329 Reg Division
101st Airborne Division
1944-1982-1989

Howard Manorie
A Co 505th Para Regt T.
Ste Mère Église
6 June 1944
82nd Div.

Clarence Hester
2nd Bn 506 Pcht Inf
Battalion 53
Sacramento California

George J. Toob Jr. 101
Los Angeles Calif.
5E2 Battalion

John Jay Ginter Jr / S/Sgt John Ginter
on 5-6 dropped a stick of the
506th Parachute Infantry Regiment
of the 101st Airborne Division
at 1:15 am June 6 1944 at nearby
Sainte Marie du Mont
92nd Troop Carrier Squadron
based at Upottery England
74 Nichols Avenue
Stamford Connecticut
06905 U.S.A.
John J. Ginter Jr.   Gene Cook
9 June 1989   "B" 506 PIR
                      101st

Colonel Russell L
82nd Bn. Inf Reg

F/O Eaton
P.F.F. Marked your 6 June
target in this area.
G. Eaton

Colonel William R. Miller
D-Day 6 June 44 with
4th Infantry Division 21/7/90

H. Bryant
116 HAA Reg. 70. 6.

Charles T. Wade 4-4-89
81st Navy C.B. Bat.
Tyler Texas

FADING KILLING FIELDS

BRIDGES AND RIVERS played vital roles as targets for destruction or capture, and as demarcation lines. As such, these landmarks often became killing fields. Today, the past is fading, retouched by pastoral brush strokes. The river *Merderet,* running innocently through the marsh (opposite top), marked the edge of the airborne drop zone. Flooded by the Germans—in places to the width of a mile—the river became the cold grave for hundreds of men landing off target.

BULLET HOLES are still visible in the walls of the bridge at La Fière (bottom right), where ten men from Able Company (1st/505th) were killed before the defenders surrendered—eight Germans raised their hands, twenty lay lifeless.

AFTER THE BATTLE came the task of burying the dead. American paratroops are wrapped in the silk of their parachutes (right center). German POWs dig graves opposite (bottom far right). The bodies of dead Germans are a gruesome sight on the next page (bottom near right).

Most westerly of the five invasion beaches, Utah was first to be assaulted, with the initial wave touching down at 0630. The men, selected from 4th U.S. Infantry Division, were untried in battle. Luckily, due to a strong current they landed four thousand yards off course, at La Madeleine, a moderately defended hamlet. It took just a few hours to cross the German lines and initiate the advance inland. The cost in lives was less than two hundred. Even today, Utah is untouched—except by the hand of nature—with the brutal edifices of concrete still dotting its lonely, windswept dunes.

ALIVE, WITH A LITTLE BIT OF LUCK

THE FIRST BATTLE facing the force heading toward the shore (twenty craft, each holding thirty men) was with seasickness. Four-foot waves, whipped up by eighteen-knot winds, tossed the landing barges like small toys, swamping them and leaving the men wading in water and vomit.

MASSIVE AIR ATTACKS (the planes swept in just above the waves, dropping their bombs with deadly precision) had all but obliterated the defenses at La Madeleine. Luckily, it was on this sector the Americans landed, having lost their bearings due to a strong current. The planned target sector was strongly defended and might have become a killing ground like Omaha Beach.

A FEW MACHINE GUNS opened up, but the losses were light. Next page (top), an MG42 fires furiously in a pre-D-Day photo. Bottom, the first wave lands. Top, medics attend to wounded.

SKELETAL GHOSTS, their firing apertures gaping emptily, remain while the waves still roll in as they did on that fateful day (color photos).

CRACKING THE CONCRETE

AFTER A MAD DASH across 800 yards of tidal banks that afforded no protection, the first wave reached the safety of a concrete wall the Germans had built at the edge of the dunes.

THEIR FIRST TASK was to breach this wall, using explosives. Tanks equipped with dozer blades then proceeded to establish roads leading out from the beach—one such exit can be seen opposite (bottom). The photo was taken just a few hours after the initial landing. Note that the swimming Shermans are still on the beach, pounding away at bunkers and pillboxes.

THE SCARS OF THE BARRAGE are still visible—a direct hit (right) cracked the concrete, baring the reinforcing rods and barely missing a ventilation shaft. The gunners soon discovered that the walls were impenetrable. Only a shot through the aperture could silence the gun.

A PERIMETER FENCE of barbed wire surrounded the strongpoints—remnants can still be seen in the dunes of Utah Beach (opposite).

SECRET WEAPON STRIKES OUT

A mini-tank, the Goliath, was Hitler's secret weapon on the beaches. Wire guided, propelled by a small two-stroke engine, and able to carry 220 pounds of explosives, it was hailed as the ultimate tank killer. Eight units were on hand in the sector where the Americans landed—at the crucial moment, however, all of them failed to start.

OUT OF THE SAND, INTO THE SWAMP

THE SIGHT OF SWIMMING TANKS rising menacingly from the sea was too much for the defenders—they raised their arms in surrender. Pictured on this page (bottom), prisoners in a cage of barbed wire await transport to England.

THE SWAMPY LOWLAND behind the beaches had been flooded on orders from Rommel. As the invaders moved out of the sand and into the soggy fields, they became bogged down. Only one dry road led inland—it had to be cleared for the arrival of troops and vehicles waiting off-shore. At the top of the page, infantry and tanks advance wearily, passing a dead German at the roadside. On opposite page (bottom), an advance party maps strategy in the courtyard of a farm near Varreville. Cows were numerous and innocent victims of the aerial bombardment.

A RUSTY GERMAN GUN points its barrel toward the beach at low tide (opposite top). To the right (center), a Tobruk—a concrete manhole topped by a machine gun or a tank turret.

BURIAL GROUND ON THE BEACH

GERMAN GUNS, firing from the Azeville and Crisbecq batteries, kept heaping destruction on Utah Beach for several days. Below, a truck and its driver are victims of a deadly projectile. Opposite (bottom) the scene on D-Day Plus Two.

THE PRIMARY SALVAGE operation on the D-Day beaches was undertaken by the Allies in 1945. At this time the majority of wreckage was removed and sold to scrap merchants. Then came the treasure hunters—today a few relics remain, the most prominent being the carcass of a landing craft visible at low tide (opposite top).

STILL A BURIAL GROUND, its bottomless sand banks hiding countless large and small objects, Utah Beach continues to yield mementos from its poignant past. Most of these finds are made by local fishermen. On this page (bottom left), the radial power plant of a landing craft, a truck engine languishing beside the remnants of the anti-tank wall (right), and the twisted steel plate from a ship (small photo opposite).

96

SAME BUNKER, DIFFERENT TIMES

THE ATLANTIC WALL relied on a three-tier system of installations. The first was a chain of radar stations—neutralized before D-Day. The second was a network of artillery batteries, with large-caliber, long-range cannons, protected by bunkers. Located away from the beaches, they targeted enemy shipping. All were bombed, but their impenetrability left them largely intact.

THE THIRD LINE consisted of a series of bunkers located on the beaches, concentrated around strongpoints called *Wiederstandsnesten*.

IN THESE PHOTOS, the camera shows the same bunker—a part of *Wiederstandsnest 7*— just north of where the Americans landed, then and now. It held an 88mm cannon—seen from the rear (opposite bottom), surrounded by the debris of war. Note in the large color photo how today the bunker is slowly being devoured by sand. In the small color photo, sunset announces the arrival of high tide on Utah Beach—the end of a long day, much like the one on June 6, 1944.

EERIE VESTIGES OF EPIC STRUGGLE

598 TONS OF BOMBS rained down on the Crisbecq battery—located four miles inland—beginning at six o'clock on D-Day morning. The four 210mm guns—one is seen opposite (far right) after its capture—had a reach of 45 miles and were serious threats to the invasion forces.

THE BOMBARDMENT did not put the guns out of action. As soon as the distant silhouettes of Allied warships became visible, the battery opened fire, sinking one destroyer. The view from the battery can be seen in the photo on this page (top). The color photo opposite shows the same view today, with the roofs of Crisbecq in the foreground and the sea beyond the haze.

THE GERMAN GARRISON, 400 men strong, repelled repeated efforts to capture the battery. Not until D-Day Plus Six, after an epic struggle, did the Germans give up, leaving many dead. The photo opposite (bottom near right) shows one of the guns from inside its casemate, with victims of the fighting laid out on the floor.

INACCESSIBLE AND INCREDIBLY PRISTINE

THE CONCRETE STRUCTURES of *Batterie Azeville* are incredibly well preserved, perhaps due to local climate conditions and its secluded location on jealously guarded private ground. Its four guns, set in bunkers of a unique design, were 105mm Schneiders with a reach of 19 miles—aimed at the beaches rather than ships.

THE CAMOUFLAGE PAINTING (opposite bottom) was a most creative touch. Note that, judging from the pockmarked windows, American gunners were indeed fooled. Note also the unique observation post on the roof, with its 37mm *Flak* gun. The color picture (opposite top) shows the same bunker today. On this page (top), the remains of a machine-gun mount. At the bottom, a look inside another bunker. The hatch leads to a tunnel and underground storage.

THE BATTLESHIP *Nevada*—two of its huge guns ablaze (right)—bombarded the battery. No hits were scored, but the 170 men garrisoned there must shave been shaking in their boots.

A HANDFUL OF HEROES

IN THE MIDST OF THE MAYHEM there were soldiers who kept their cool. These men, a handful here, a handful there, managed to fight their way through the beach defenses and up the bluff to the plateau, where they gathered in larger groups, some mounting attacks on the Germans from the rear, others moving inland.

SHIELDS AGAINST BULLETS were found on the boulder-strewn approach to the beach at sector Charlie (color photo right), located on the easternmost edge of the front. Opposite, the cliff rises from the same beach. It was here that another handful of men (from the 2d Ranger Battalion) climbed the rock under cover of thick smoke to attack the German defenders on top.

IN SHOCK from fear and exhaustion, men from the 1st Battalion, 116th Infantry, hug the beach below the cliffs at the western edge of the front (black and white photos). Even here, groups of men climbed to the top—the victory at Omaha Beach was won by the few and the brave.

SCENES FROM AFTER THE STORM

AN EERIE STILLNESS hangs over sector Dog Green (bottom). A lone GI contemplates the gruesome scene of a few days earlier, when the surf was lined with the bodies of his comrades. Further back, the jagged hull of a landing craft juts out above the tide, while in the foreground the long barrel of an 88mm still points menacingly.

A FEVERISH ACTIVITY at sector Easy Green fills the photograph on opposite page (top). An armada of ships is bringing in reinforcements and vitally needed materiel. In the foreground, the skeleton of an unfinished German pillbox.

THE NAVAL BARRAGE (destroyers moved to within 1,000 yards) played a crucial role in turning the tide on D-Day. To the right, damage inflicted on the wall of a German fortification.

THE FIRE FROM MACHINE GUNS was the most deadly. Next page (bottom), the mounting platform of an MG42 is charmingly overgrown with the obliviousness of time. Before the battle was over, one German had fired 12,000 rounds.

FIGHTING FOR A FOOTHOLD

THE FIRST REPORTS from Omaha Beach were alarming. Aboard the *USS Augusta,* steaming twelve miles offshore, General Omar Bradley contemplated redirecting the landings to Utah Beach. Fearing that this might cause dangerous congestion, he decided instead to hold back materiel and send in more men. The pressure became too much for the defenders. By noon the tide had turned, and the fight for a secure foothold moved inland. Opposite (bottom), a column has halted to probe the road for mines. Now materiel could be brought in (top), and prisoners (right center) could be rounded up.

THE PEACEFUL COUNTRYSIDE, opposite (top), hid an invisible enemy—it was the first taste of the bloody hedge-row war. This particular lane leads to a spot where the Germans stored guns moved from *Pointe du Hoc*. At the bottom of this page, a country house destroyed by bombs was never repaired, and a farmer's gate still bears witness to the war that passed long ago.

RANGERS CLIMB THE ROPES

ONE OF THE MOST DARING operations on D-Day was mounted by 195 men of the 2d Rangers. Their target was a German battery built atop *Pointe du Hoc,* a precipice with 100-foot walls. The color photograph depicts the narrow strip of beach where the rangers landed in eight small craft. A ninth craft sank along the way.

SIX HUGE GUNS threatened both Utah and Omaha. Aerial bombardment had turned the battery, garrisoned by 210 Germans, into a moonscape—but damage to the guns was unknown. Within thirty minutes the attackers, scaling the cliffs on ropes and ladders (opposite page), were at the top, immediately engaging the enemy. The Rangers took fifteen casualties on the beach, seventy-five more in the ensuing fighting, but found the gun emplacements empty (right).

LARGE SHELLS, detonated by a pull-type device and fitted with a short-delay fuse, were found hanging along the cliff walls (bottom right). On the left, a primitive German flame thrower.

THE FACE OF WAR FROZEN IN TIME

THE BATTLEGROUND at *Pointe du Hoc* has been preserved. A carpet of grass softens up the ragged contours of the bomb craters, but the scarred face of war is there to see. Opposite (top), a view from the point of the promontory.

A RUBBLE OF TWISTED METAL (right), shows the force of the bombardment. A GI is dwarfed by a crater (bottom left). Next to this, a cannon mount thrown far from its foundation.

NAVAL SHELLING, first from the battleship *Texas* and then from the destroyer *Satterlee*, finished what the aerial bombardment had left. A bunker (below) has been hit right on target.

A NETWORK OF TUNNELS (top right) kept the defenders alive—they came out to fight the Rangers with a vengeance. The fact that no guns were found at first made the costly operation seem in vain. However, a patrol soon discovered the guns two miles inland, sighted on Utah Beach. Grenades were thrown down their barrels, which effectively put them out of action.

116

HITLER'S CREATIONS COLLAPSE

HITLER HIMSELF originated not only the principal concept of the Atlantic Wall, but also its individual components. Thus, a number of the construction plans for the various bunkers and pillboxes were based on the Führer's own sketches, which he worked on late at night.

THE FISHING TOWN of Grandcamp—ten miles west of Omaha Beach—was passed over as a landing site by the invasion planners. Thus the fortifications do not carry the usual scars of battle. Nevertheless, Hitler's creations are finally showing signs of collapsing, their foundations being washed out to sea. The waves have nearly swallowed a pillbox (bottom) while a bunker (right center) leans precariously into the surf.

BEACH OBSTACLES had been placed along the shore, despite the presence of treacherous underwater rocks. Stakes topped by mines (top) were common, as were the tetrahedras. These rusty contraptions (opposite) are the only ones to have escaped the scrap-iron merchants.

GOLD BEACH

For the 0725 assault on Gold by the British 50th Infantry Division, planners had picked a stretch between La Rivière and Le Hamel. Stubborn resistance, with fire coming from concrete emplacements hiding powerful 88-mm guns, as well as vacation homes converted into fortified machine gun nests, slowed the advance. The picturesque town of Arromanche was not taken until the next day. This was the site of Overlord's trump card, the artificial Mulberry harbor. Remnants of its caissons—towed across the Channel—survive as reminders of a commitment to victory that knew no limits.

CONQUERING THE WALL OF STEEL AND CONCRETE

SIX ROWS OF MINES had been sown by the German defenders on the wide beach at Le Hamel. Ominous signs (opposite bottom right), warned villagers to stay off the inviting sand.

THE DEADLY TASK of clearing a path for the Allied assault—spearheaded by two thousand men from the 231st Infantry Brigade (Hampshires and Dorsets)—was left to the engineers and the flail tanks. Despite their success, the attackers were pinned down by savage machine-gun fire. Losses were heavy. Later waves of invaders had an easier time—men from the 56th Infantry Brigade landed in orderly columns (right top).

THE GERMAN DEFENDERS, 270 loyal *Wehrmacht* officers and one thousand Russian conscripts of dubious quality, were clustered around pillboxes—such as the one seen opposite (bottom left), hiding a 50-mm antitank gun.

THE TEETH OF TIME chew away at a casemate east of Asnelles (the two color photos), severely damaged by naval bombardment.

LINGERING MEMENTOS FROM LONG AGO

THE WESTERN SECTOR of the five-mile front designated as Gold Beach was assaulted by troops from the 69th Infantry Brigade (East Yorkshires and Green Howards). Although faced with strong German fire, the Green Howards moved swiftly across the beach and advanced inland, while elements of the East Yorkshires were held up by stubborn resistance at the village of La Rivière. The photo opposite (bottom), was taken later in the day when the beaches had been cleared for arrival of reinforcements.

BLOWING UP BEACH OBSTACLES was a job for the engineers (top right)—here seen demolishing iron hedgehogs in the foreground and wooden log ramps further out. The nasty contraptions were underwater at high tide.

REMNANTS OF THE ARTIFICIAL harbor, which lay beached on the shore from Asnelles to Arromanches (the color shots show them at high and low tides), remind both visitors and local fishermen of a less peaceful time long ago.

FLOATING WONDER OF THE WAR

NO LANDINGS TOOK PLACE on the beach at Arromanches. The Allies had other plans for the small town with its sheltered location—it was to be the site of the artificial Mulberry harbor. The photo opposite shows Arromanches on a day much like that of fifty years ago, with the waves breaking violently against the sea wall.

A FIELD GUN of World War I vintage (77mm) protected the eastern slope—remnants of the gun can still be seen (right). The western edge was defended by a smaller casemated gun —the 47-mm Skoda is also still in place (top).

ON D-DAY PLUS SIX, the artificial harbor had seen as many as 326,000 men and 54,000 vehicles traverse its floating roadways. To the far right (opposite), an aerial view captures the construction stage, with a row of sunken block ships calming the waves. The color photo shows the caissons as they appear today at low tide. To the right, an overview of Arromanches taken from the German Strongpoint at Saint-Côme.

126

FACES AND FACADES OF CHANGE

THE BITTER BATTLE for Arromanches left only six houses intact. As many as forty-three were completely destroyed, while 180 suffered partial damage. D-Day had begun early in the morning, with Allied bombers assaulting the Longues battery west of town. Later there had been devastating German mortar fire, and in the afternoon the British had attacked, forcing the 600-man strong German garrison to surrender.

A SET OF UNIQUE PHOTOS, taken a few days later—before the Mulberry harbor altered the scene—illustrate the changes brought on by the passing of time. To the right (top), one of the town's most striking houses, battle scarred. The color photos show the same building today —home to *Hotel La Marine* (the author was a guest in the second-story corner room, from which one of the shutters once dangled precariously).

FACES OF THE OLD, seen on the spot where tourists now enjoy the view, show mixed emotions—fifteen families mourned their dead.

BATTLE OF THE BEHEMOTHS

A CLASSIC ARTILLERY BATTLE, pitting no less than five Allied cruisers—with its five dozen large-caliber guns—against the German four-gun battery near the shore at Longues, began at daybreak on D-Day and lasted until dark.

BUILT ON A PLATEAU 198 feet above sea level, the battery overlooked all of the Bay of Seine. Its 150-mm guns, manufactured by the Skoda firm in Pilsen, Czechoslovakia, had a range of over twelve miles—and thus threatened Allied landing operations from Omaha to Juno. All four cannons were protected by huge concrete casemates. The stepped upper portion of the embrasure allowed the barrel to be raised to its maximum, yet minimized the size of the aperture.

WORK ON THE BATTERY had begun in September 1943. On D-Day, the bunker housing the sophisticated fire-direction gear was not yet operational—had it been, the effect of the shelling could have been devastating. As it was, the menacing guns at Longues scored mostly near-hits.

FREEDOM FOR THE FISHING FLEET

EARLY MORNING FOG over Port-en-Bessin brings to mind the smoke screen laid by naval gunfire during the battle for the town fifty years ago. A close study of the houses lining the harbor in the photos opposite (the historic picture captures a Bren gun carrier crawling off an LCT), shows how little the facades have changed.

FOR CENTURIES fishing was the source of income in Port-en-Bessin. This came to an end during the war, when the fleet was confined to port. It was a day of celebration when the Allied liberation set the fleet free. Pictured to the right (bottom), the *Tricolore* flies from mast tops. Today's color photos are taken on the same spot.

THE SECLUDED PORT, surrounded by its long arms of protective jetties, was chosen as a termination point (right center) for PLUTO (Pipe Line Under The Ocean)—four parallel lines (for gasoline, oil, water, and reserve), resting on the Channel floor. British terminals were located on the south-east coast of the Isle of Wight.

The Canadian 3d Infantry Division, spearheaded by regiments with noble names like Queen's Own Rifles and Royal Winnipeg Rifles, touched down thirty minutes late, at 0755. The delay gave the Germans time to organize their resistance, which centered on the seaside resorts of Courseulles, Bernières and Saint Aubin. But determined to avenge the Dieppe disaster, the Canadians fought hard. At day's end, they had put ashore twenty thousand men, and had pushed further inland than any other invasion force—regrettably at a cost of more than one thousand dead and wounded.

CANADIANS BRAVE THE BULLETS

FOUR-FOOT WAVES made the run into shore an agonizing ordeal for the four hundred men from Canada's 7th Infantry Brigade (A, B, C, and D Companies, Winnipeg Rifles). Waiting to turn their distress into a murderous hell were one hundred Germans (716th Infantry Division, 736th Regiment) armed to the teeth (right).

BEHIND THE FRONT LINE, the Germans were not so well equipped—most of the artillery pieces were horse drawn (opposite bottom).

A TRAGIC ORDEAL awaited the B Company, landing at La Valette where pre-assault bombing had been lacking. Only one fourth of the men were still standing when tanks of the 1st Hussars finally managed to zero in on the deadly enemy fire from a concrete casemate (opposite top).

LATER IN THE DAY, with the beaches cleared, reinforcements poured in—intriguingly documented by an aerial photo (bottom right).

A BULLET-SCARRED SIGN (top of the page), stands beside the road to Gray-sur-Mer.

CLEARING A DEADLY OBSTACLE COURSE

SUPPORTED BY TANKS, which had swum in from 2,000 yards (five of nineteen sank in the rough seas), Canadians from the Regina Rifle Regiment (A and B Companies) hit the beaches of Courseulles at 0825. In addition to the usual hedgehog obstacles, the Germans had installed their C-elements—monstrous iron gates (top), removed from antitank defenses in Belgium.

THE EFFECT of the C-elements, which were mined, was devastating—as can be seen opposite (top), where damaged landing craft drift in the high tide, smashing into remnants of the sea wall.

STONES FROM THE WALL are still found on the beach (opposite bottom). Other relics include a 50-mm gun (one of three such weapons used in the defense of Courseulles), its shield pierced by the deadly projectile from a tank.

THE GERMANS, like this prisoner (bottom right), were often very young. The scene to the far right shows after-battle devastation in a beach house occupied by German officers.

REMEMBERING THE QUEEN'S OWN RIFLES

LIVES CAME TO AN END in the shattering flash of an exploding grenade, or the brief, burning penetration of a whizzing bullet—both sides suffered heavy losses when four hundred Canadians of the Queen's Own Rifles (Companies A and B) landed at Bernières. The defenders, about one hundred strong, manned a formidable Strongpoint directly in the attackers' path. To the right (top), Canadian dead washed up in the surf. On opposite page (bottom far right), German dead at the entrance to their trenches.

A HEROIC ACTION by three Canadians who neutralized the main pillbox (seen opposite bottom left), using grenades and sub-machine guns finally gave the edge to the invaders.

THE SACRIFICE for freedom is remembered everywhere in Bernières—to the right (bottom), the Canadian flag flies in dusky evening light.

ANOTHER RELIC (opposite top), is a British AVRE, firing an awesome 290-mm concrete-cracking mortar nicknamed "Flying Dustbin."

THE BIG HOUSE ON THE BEACH

SINKING LANDING CRAFT, blown up by mines and mortar rounds, forced crews of all but five LCAs of the volunteer French-Canadian *Le Régiment de la Chaudière* to discard their heavy equipment and swim ashore. Two of the five unharmed crews are landing opposite (bottom).

A BIG HALF-TIMBERED HOUSE, still standing (below right), became a landmark for the 9th Canadian Infantry that touched down later in the morning. The enemy resistance had been neutralized by then, but the high tide gave little room for maneuver (above). The narrow strip of sand was soon clogged by men and materiel.

EQUIPPED WITH BICYCLES, the infantry forged ahead, pedaling through the deserted countryside, capturing villages often held only by snipers. Backed up by tanks, the 9th rolled on until halted by a solid enemy front just short of their D-Day objective. If it had all seemed so comparatively easy to most of the men, the days and weeks ahead would be a nightmare.

STREET FIGHTING IN SAINT-AUBIN

TOWERING OVER THE BEACH at Saint-Aubin was a formidable resistance nest hiding a 50-mm cannon, complemented by four machine guns in fortified houses. The cannon stopped two tanks before a Royal Marine Centaur, an AVRE, and a Fort Garry House Sherman silenced it.

THE PILLBOX still stands (opposite top). Its cannon (bottom right), was fitted with a muzzle brake, permitting the use of heavier charges.

STUBBORN ENEMY fire kept the North Shore Regiment—landing at 0740—pinned down on the beach. The arrival of No. 48 Royal Marines eased the situation, and in a bypass move the combined force attacked from the rear. To the right (center), Canadians take cover. The roof of the pillbox can be seen at the end of the street. On opposite page (bottom), a Duplex Drive Sherman (swimming tank) rumbles through debris from the ferocious fighting.

A ROAD SIGN (top), posted in 1938, shows slipshod repairs of numerous bullet strikes.

IN THE EYE OF THE STORM

ABBEY ARDENNE, a showcase of Gothic style—located west of Caen—fell into disrepair during the nineteenth century. As fate would have it, World War II thrust the Abbey into the eye of the storm, causing further degeneration.

DURING THE OCCUPATION the Abbey became a Resistance center, its gardens serving as hiding places for weapons. Both Roland and Francine Vico, who had lived in the Abbey gatehouse since the twenties, were arrested by the Gestapo for their underground activities.

THE INVASION brought repeated waves of destruction—the first on the 7th and 8th of June when 12th SS fought the Canadians. Artillery bombardment caused continuous damage until Montgomery's troops finally captured Caen in July and forced the Germans to retreat. The black-and-white photos show the carnage at that time. The color photos depict the Abbey today. Restoration, which has continued for decades, is now at a standstill due to lack of funds.

ROMMEL RETURNS, HITLER HESITATES

SHOCKED BY THE NEWS from Normandy, Rommel—still at home in Germany—boards his car for a furious race to the front. Hitler, given the news when awakened at ten o'clock, keeps his appointments. Later, after initially holding back the panzer, he finally issues marching orders.

ON D-DAY PLUS ONE, 12th SS Panzer joins 21st Panzer, setting up headquarters in Abbey Ardenne. A rare photo (opposite far right), shows Fritz Witt, commander 21st Panzer (center), Max Wünsche, commander 12th Panzer (right), and Kurt Meyer, commander 25th Panzer Grenadier Regiment, crossing a courtyard at the Abbey.

THE TURRETS, from which Meyer directed his tanks have been restored (color photos). A narrow stairway leads skyward (opposite top).

PANTHER TANKS led the German attack. This page (top), a *Panther* under way, complete with camouflage and infantry. When Allied planes shot fuel trucks into flames, Meyer kept his tanks going via a *Kübelwagen* shuttle (bottom).

MURDEROUS ANIMOSITY

"ARROGANT BRUTES" was how a Canadian officer described the German Panzer troops—particularly those of the 12th SS, the *Hitlerjugend* (Hitler Youth). The face of a soldier at Abbey Ardenne (opposite top), expresses ferocious zeal as well as fanatical loathing for the enemy.

THE MURDEROUS ANIMOSITY reached a peak during the German counterattack—led by Kurt Meyer's *Hitlerjugend*. The Canadians, with Highlanders and Regina Rifles up front, moved against the Carpiquet airport when ambushed by Meyer's men. The battle raged into the night, when both sides retreated, taking prisoners. The Germans brought theirs to the Abbey, where nineteen were murdered execution style. Their remains were found after the war in shallow graves—clubbed and shot to death. To the right (bottom), two Canadians under interrogation.

THE NAVE of the thirteenth-century Abbey (to the right), has been partially restored, but still shows wounds from the barrage of bullets.

SWORD BEACH

One hundred seventy-seven Free-French joined with the Green Berets of British 3d Infantry Division–fortified by accompanying bagpipes–in the assault on Sword. Landing at 0725, 1st Commando pushed eastward, taking Ouistreham, while 4th Commando, pushing westward, failed to link up with Canadian forces at Juno. This left a dangerous gap between beachheads, which the German panzer attempted to exploit, but failed. Half a century later, like dogged reminders, a single row of Dragon Teeth (concrete anti-tank obstacles) still stands watch among the changing-huts.

RIDING THE WAVES OF QUEEN WHITE

BRITISH DRAGOON GUARDS, charging out of the surf in their mine-clearing flail tanks, were the first to assault Sword Beach. Follow-up waves arrived twenty minutes apart: 1st South Lancashire crossed the beach with few casualties and moved off toward Hermanville; Suffolk Regiment set out for Colleville; 2nd East Yorkshire lost two hundred men before heading toward Ouistreham. Opposite (top), a bird's-eye view of the initial landings at sector Queen White.

THE HAZE OF BATTLE hangs heavy over the beach when Royal Marine Commandos wade ashore (this page bottom), proudly favoring their green berets over protective helmets.

THE DESTROYER BEAGLE (right center), was one of many warships steaming close to the beach, giving fire support when needed.

WAVES WASH ASHORE on Queen White today (opposite bottom). A bullet-pierced helmet (far right), and a Lee-Enfield rifle (top), are among the many relics relinquished by the sand.

THE STUCCO STILL TELLS THE STORY

ONE HOUR AFTER THE LANDING, the engineers had managed to open the first of half a dozen gaps in the fortified sea wall, allowing vehicles to move off the heavily congested beach. A photograph (opposite bottom), snapped just a few hours later at the most westerly gap in La Brèche, shows an AVRE of the 79th Armoured Division (left), and Bren carriers of the 2nd Middlesex Regiment, preparing to move inland.

ALTHOUGH RELATIVELY UNDAMAGED, the house in the background shows scars from the fighting. Heavy machine gun salvos have hammered holes in stucco, stones, and bricks. The color photograph on this page shows the same building today, its damage skillfully repaired yet still discernible, especially in stones and bricks.

CLOSE SCRUTINY of facades along a narrow street in Lion-sur-Mer yielded the scene opposite (top). These repairs have been less successful—some of the fillings have fallen out. Damage to the shutters was left unrepaired.

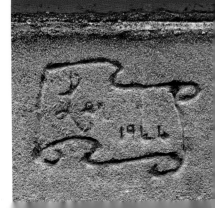

SHERMANS VERSUS MK IV SPECIALS

RACING TOWARD THE SEA in the late afternoon, a formation of 124 German tanks was potentially the most serious threat to the Allied beachhead on D-Day. If pulled off, the maneuver would widen the gap between Juno and Sword, splitting the front. Opposite page (bottom), a Sherman crew rests before taking on the enemy.

THE MK IV SPECIAL was more than a match for the Sherman whose frontal armor it could penetrate at 1,000 yards. A Sherman was unable to inflict the same damage at 100 yards. Nevertheless, the Shermans halted the enemy at Hill 61, crippling seventy Mk IVs (this page top). Just six enemy tanks slipped through to the coast, only to turn back for fear of being cut off.

THE SHERMAN came in many guises, the most intriguing being the swimming DD (Duplex Drive) version—one of which is seen opposite (top), escorting Royal Marines on their way to capture Ouistreham. To the right, a closeup of a Sherman salvaged from the bottom of the sea.

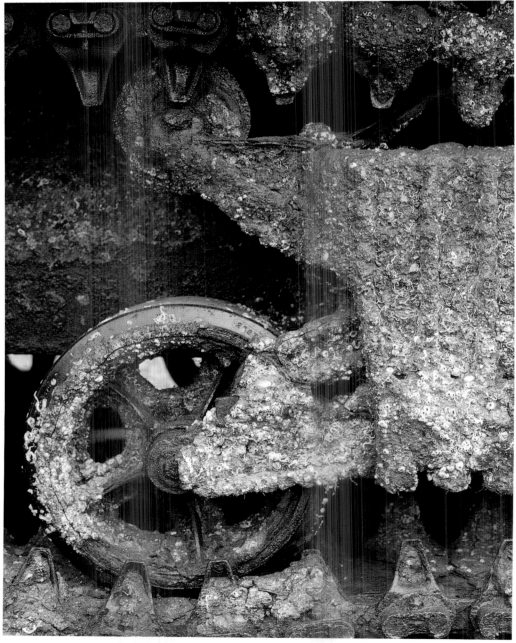

TRAPPED IN A TIME WARP

A SPLENDID MANSION, devastated by the fury of the invasion assault, still stands as it did on that fateful day, trapped in a time warp—the roof pierced by artillery shells, the doors and windows blown out from the force of the concussions, the facade pockmarked from mortar and machine gun barrages, the rooms littered with debris—only the irreverent graffiti brings the entranced viewer back to reality.

THE FIRST VICTIMS of the fighting on the beaches were buried in temporary graves in the walled gardens of this mansion, located in Colleville-sur-Mer. The tiny town, which found itself right in the path of the fierce fighting, gave homage to the liberators by changing its name to Colleville-Montgomery after the war.

A BRITISH COMMANDO (right top), pokes the barrel of a Bren through a puncture in a wall—waiting for the enemy to appear in his sights, while a German soldier (opposite bottom), stands at the ready behind an MG-42.

TWENTY INCHES OF IRON, SIX FEET OF CONCRETE

THE MORNING SUN rises over Riva-Bella (opposite top). No troops landed here—the invaders instead advanced along the coast road.

POWERFUL GUNS were set in open mounts. Just prior to D-Day, Rommel ordered them removed—they were too easy prey for bombers. The 155-mm pieces were French Schneiders (opposite bottom), and had a range of ten miles.

AN IRON BELL (right bottom), tops a bunker in Ouistreham harbor. The walls—twenty inches of massive iron—enclosed one observer looking through a periscope, and two machine guns.

STRONGPOINT HILLMAN, up the road from Colleville, played a vital role on D-Day, its garrison of Grenadiers holding up the British advance, preventing capture of Caen. Concrete bunkers with six-foot walls remain (top).

THE TALL MAST of the French battleship *Courbet,* deliberately sank as a blockship, forms the focusing point of a photo taken on June 7 (right center), found in a German archive.

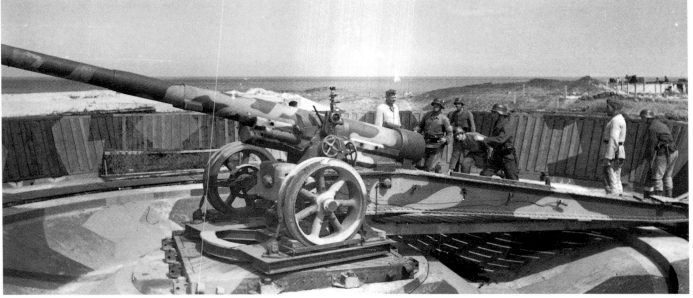

The Allies' complete superiority in the air was a key to their success. Spitfires and Typhoons began to operate from Normandy already on D-Day Plus One, flying out of strips that were nothing more than straight pieces of grassy ground extending more than 1,800 feet. Below, a Spitfire is being refueled and rearmed.

FLOWERS FOR THE FALLEN

THREE THOUSAND LIVES were lost in the Allied landing operations on D-Day. German casualties were countless. But regardless of nationality, death was always the same—final. Makeshift graves were dug in orchards and fields. Mounds of soil, bunches of flowers, and wooden crosses marked the temporary sites.

PERMANENT RESTING PLACES were located after the war. One of the largest among the British cemeteries is found in Ranville. At the top of this page, a wreath is placed at the foot of a monument to 6th Airborne. Ranville is also a burial site for Free French (opposite).

TEN THOUSAND GERMANS are laid to rest at La Cambe. One of the simple stones embedded in the wide, manicured lawns carries the name of Michael Wittman, leading tank ace of the war, who met his maker when faced by five Shermans.

AMERICAN FALLEN are buried in Saint-Laurent—a moving sight with its meticulously aligned rows of 9,385 white marble crosses.

It was the dream and determination of Charles de Gaulle that led to formation of the Free French, an exile army of French patriots. A small but brave force of Free French took part in the D-Day invasion, leaving eleven comrades dead. In the village of Amfreville, locals were happy (below) to find their own countrymen among the liberators.

The unconquerability of the Atlantic Wall was indeed a myth, the fighting ability of the German soldier was not. British and Canadians felt the ferocity of Hitler's elite forces at Caen. Teenagers still, they kept the city from Monty's men for a month. Bradley's Americans fared a bit better, capturing Cherbourg after three weeks. It required men like Patton and battles like Falaise, however, to break the enemy's back and clear the way for final victory. But it was on the beaches that the destiny of the Third Reich was decided. June 6, D-Day, was indeed the Day of Decision.

BEYOND THE BEACHES

THE DAWN OF DEFEAT

President Roosevelt, pictured on June 6 (below), struck a note of caution at his press conference: "You just don't walk to Berlin." Leading the nation in prayer, his thoughts went to the men on the beaches: "Lead them straight and true. Give strength to their arms, stoutness to their hearts."

The evening of June 5 had been unpleasant on the Normandy coast, with heavy rains, strong winds. Despite the hostile weather Major Hans von Luck, the cautious, seasoned commander of the 125th Panzer Grenadiers, 21st Panzer Division, had dispatched one of his crack battalions on a night training exercise.

Now, with midnight nearing, von Luck sat at a table, maps spread before him, waiting for his men to return. The simply furnished farm house stood at the edge of an orchard near the main road to Paris, outside Bellengreville, a village six miles east of Caen and ten miles from the stretch of coast the Allies called Sword Beach—toward which, unbeknownst to von Luck, an armada of enemy landing ships steamed stealthily.

Around midnight Major von Luck became aware of the roar of low-flying aircraft. The thought that it was a prelude to the long-awaited invasion did not cross his mind. After all, commanders had been told that the storm prevented the launching of an amphibious operation. A few days of much-needed rest had been urged. In fact, divisional commanders had scheduled war games at Rennes for June 6. Most of the invited brass had already left their various

LONDON LISTENS AND HOLDS ITS BREATH

In offices and factories, work had to wait while Londoners listened
to news bulletins on the radio. In Parliament, Churchill
reported the encouraging news with his customary wit. In the streets,
pedestrians stopped to talk and read the papers (above).
And, perched outside his cage, an unlikely hero posed proudly for the
photographer (left). Gustave was the first to return with
a message from the beaches. Released at 0830—facing 60 mph
head winds—he landed at his Royal Air Force pigeon
coop four hours and forty-six minutes later.

Churchill (below) surveys the beaches from the deck of a destroyer on June 12. Five days later, Hitler (top right, with Field Marshal von Kluge) visits the front for the first and last time. Montgomery (below right) came ashore on June 8. Dapper and confident, Eisenhower (far right) during a five-day tour in mid-June.

headquarters, eager to enjoy an evening away from the tension of constant readiness.

When the roar began to grow in intensity, von Luck walked across the room to one of its small windows. Sweeping aside the curtains he found that the sky—which had cleared, with only low clouds moving swiftly across a full moon—was lighted by flares and anti-aircraft fire. The radiant bursts sent flashes of yellow and red light across his face, its chiseled features suddenly showing the strain of apprehension, disbelief.

At that very moment the telephone rang. His adjutant, calling from the command post in the village, informed him that British paratroops and gliders were landing in the area.

Standing orders were not to take action without explicit clearance from superiors. Major Von Luck instructed his adjutant to place the regiment on full alert, and to inform divisional headquarters immediately. His forward battalion had counterattacked on its own, and was already bringing in prisoners for questioning. As the Major hurried to the command post, he worried about his other battalion, the one on night exercise—he had regrettably sent them out with blank ammunition.

FINALLY FREE, THE FRENCH GO WILD

De Gaulle, symbol of the struggle for a free France, returned on June 14, met by jubilant crowds. Opposite, he walks in the streets of Bayeux, and, below, speaks to the citizens of Cherbourg. Scenes like this (bottom), were played out all across France in the wake of the Allies' advance.

At daybreak, orders to counterattack had still not been received. Von Luck had learned that General Edgar Feuchtinger, the divisional commander, was in Paris on an errand of private nature. The higher-ups were still in Rennes. And Rommel, overall commander, was still with his wife in Germany.

Eager for an accurate picture of the unfolding assault, von Luck had taken up position on a high ridge to the east of Caen. Wrestling with the emotions of a growing frustration, he turned his binoculars toward the coast.

The sight overwhelmed him. Beyond the Orne estuary the horizon seemed completely filled with the awe-inspiring silhouettes of warships. The orange flames of their relentless barrage cut through the gray haze like sharp reflections of knife blades brandished in bright morning sun. Closer at hand von Luck discovered hundreds of gliders, looking like so many wing-shot birds, dotting the fields north of Ranville.

He knew the coastal defenses could simply not withstand an assault of this magnitude. Only an immediate counterattack by the panzer might save the situation. But even this last-ditch effort, von Luck became convinced as he scanned the coastline, would soon be doomed.

euchtinger arrived from Paris at seven in the morning. On the way back *he* had also witnessed the Allied armada—awesome in its overwhelming might—and was convinced the invasion was a full-scale effort. He asked that his forces be allowed to counterattack immediately. Aggressive use of the tank formations under his command would split the beachhead in two, he felt. But his request was denied.

Hitler, informed of the news from Normandy when awakened at ten in the morning, did not modify his agenda—for the customary midday conference he and his entourage motored to a castle one hour from Berchtesgaden, where he received the new Hungarian Prime Minister.

Thus it was afternoon before Hitler dealt with the Normandy situation. After first having been convinced that the shore defenses were fully up to the task of fending off the attackers, he later changed his mind and released the panzer. But it was too late—the tank columns became easy prey for Allied Typhoons and Spitfires. All that the German effort accomplished, although this would prove significant, was to prevent the British and Canadians from taking Caen.

Rommel did not reach his headquarters until ten at night. Had he been present during the

HELL AMONG THE HEDGEROWS

● ●

The Americans were ill-prepared for the bocage, where an invisible enemy lurked behind every leaf. Its narrow fields(above), cultivated for a thousand years, were surrounded by hedges that proved virtually impenetrable, forcing the tanks into narrow lanes where they—unable to traverse their turrets—became sitting ducks. Far left, a German staff car meets a column of trucks in a typical bocage lane. Above left, an M4 tank-dozer penetrates a hedgerow in a staged shot—this was not the norm. The problem was solved by Sergeant Curtis Culin, who struck upon the idea of cutting down salvaged German beach obstacles and welding them to the front of the tank (left), creating a tusk-like contraption. Thus was born the "Rhino," which earned Culin a Legion of Merit medal.

LANCASTERS, THUNDERBOLTS AND PIPER CUBS

• •

Five hundred heavy bombers, mostly Lancasters, rained destruction on Caen
during the night of July 7 (top right). A Thunderbolt fighter bomber
lands in flames (bottom right). The smallest fry of the air war was the Piper
Cub, shuttling over the front at 80 mph, spotting for the artillery.
The pilots camped wherever they landed (below).

crucial early hours, it seems safe to speculate that he would have taken action regardless of orders. Now he spent an endless, sleepless night trying to organize a counterattack which, when finally mounted, accomplished too little, too late.

On the Allied side, commanders were justly satisfied. True, the Americans at Utah and Omaha had failed to link up, as had the British and Canadians at Sword and Juno. But the beachhead was safe, the foothold secure.

Nearly 160,000 troops had been put ashore: 73,000 Americans (34,000 at Omaha, 23,000 at Utah, and 16,000 airborne), 62,000 British (25,000 at Gold, 29,000 at Sword, and 8,000 airborne), and 21,000 Canadians at Juno.

Casualties were less than expected: 10,000, of which one third were killed. As far as materiel, losses were also relatively light: two destroyers, 291 landing craft, and 127 airplanes.

Without the element of surprise the Allied invasion would most likely have failed. The storm, which caused the enemy to lower its guard, and the unexpected calm, which allowed the Allies to mount the invasion, were fortunate circumstances. Eisenhower's decision

The stream of tanks landing on the Allied beaches was endless, while the Germans could not replace theirs. A Sherman (below) emerges from the mouth of an LST. A Tiger (bottom) lies dead in the streets of Falaise, scene of the final battle, from which the Germans escaped with 67 tanks. The Allied pincer closed with the force of 2,000 tanks.

to take advantage of the break in the weather, however, was not a stroke of luck—it was tactical audacity of momentous magnitude.

Complicating the enemy's situation—on top of the uncertainty of *when* the invasion would take place—was the question of *where*.

Pas de Calais, located at the narrowest point of the Channel, was the obvious target. The second alternative, which strategists on both sides had found—based on the suitability of its beaches— was Normandy. However, this route was longer —across the Channel as well as to Berlin, the heart of Germany. Hitler's fortification and troop deployment decisions reflected this reality— Normandy was less well defended.

Fortitude, umbrella code for the operations designed to keep the Germans in the dark as to the *when* and the *where*, remains one of the great feats of military deception.

Although England's borders, with the nation being an island, could be effectively controlled, it was nevertheless incredible that all German spies entering and operating in England—about two dozen—were caught. Even more incredible was the fact that every one of these spies was convinced to turn double agent.

THE COST OF CONFLICT, THE WAGES OF WAR

• •

While the Allied's advantage in numbers of tanks, aircraft and artillery
pieces—a British 5.5-inch medium gun (left) fires into the
night—played a pivotal role in the outcome of the massive battles, when it came
to street fighting (above) it was man to man, bullet for bullet. At the end
of the Normandy campaign, German casualties stood at 240,000. The allies had
lost 65,000—nearly half of them were airmen. French civilians paid
a heavy price—tens of thousands died during air raids and from enemy
reprisals. Many did not hesitate to lay their lives on the line
in support of their liberators—a French woman (top left) keeps a
British gunner supplied with liquid refreshment.

AGONY, AND THE ACCIDENTAL VICTIM

* *

An air raid (below) wreaks havoc on St. Lo, a vital communications center that was the July 25 starting point for Cobra, Bradley's successful breakout from the Contentin peninsula. The agony of war hit the elderly hardest—some were too weak to walk (bottom), others simply chose to stay behind (opposite top).

An elaborate scheme that relied on fake radio signals—as well as dummy tanks and landing ships—tricked the enemy into believing that an Allied army was assembling opposite Pas de Calais. To lend further credence to the scheme, Patton (the one Allied general Hitler respected) was named commander of the paper army—an appointment conveniently passed on to German intelligence through the double agents.

The deception efforts culminated on the night of the invasion with activation of *Taxable* and *Glimmer.* Conceived to make German commanders believe a massive invasion armada was steaming in the direction of Pas de Calais, these operations combined a variety of measures—such as launches towing reflective balloons, and airplanes dropping aluminum strips—to create the illusion of extensive ship movements on German radar screens. To make the deception complete, as the electronic flotilla neared France, enormous loudspeakers began blaring amplified engine sounds toward the enemy coast. As it happened, wind and waves drowned out the audibles, and relaxed German security failed to interpret the visuals to the extent intended by the planners.

LOVE, AND LIFE UNDER GROUND

• •

*The city of Caen was a key to Allied advance. But the Germans
repelled Montgomery's every attack until on July 10, after
a horrible night of bombardment, the enemy began to withdraw. A
fourth of the population had evacuated beforehand, but most
stayed, finding shelter whereever possible—1,500 packed into Saint-
Étienne church, and 6,000 hid in the Fleury caves. Life under
ground was lived on the edge, the moment counting more than a
future that might not come—a young woman (left)
makes herself beautiful for her lover.*

Fortitude nevertheless accomplished its main goal—long after the Normandy landings, Hitler kept his strongest forces in the Pas de Calais area, convinced that the D-Day assault was nothing more than a diversionary operation.

General Bernard Law Montgomery, dressed in polo sweater, khaki pants and trademark black beret, sits on a folding chair in the garden of Chateau Creullet, the ancient castle near Bayeux, where his command trailer (cleverly camouflaged as a haystack) has been set up.

The general gesticulates vigorously—spreading his hands in expansive declarations, pumping them up and down, inflating accomplishments and expectations—explaining his positions to the audience before him, a group of correspondents seated on the lawn like disciples before the master. It is June 11, 1944—D-Day Plus Five—and General Montgomery presides over his first press conference after the invasion. There is much optimism, much to be pleased about.

But as the war and the weeks wore on, optimism degenerated into pessimism. The British and Canadians were stalled outside Caen, the Americans bogged down in the

MEN AND WOMEN OF THE MAQUIS

• •

The first resistance in France began in the most desolate area of the country, the "maquis"—the word became synonymous with freedom fighter. The Allied landings provided the signal for the resistance to go into open action, but D-Day began with a tragedy—ninety were executed on June 6, machine-gunned to death in the courtyard of the Caen prison. Unified under the Cross of Lorraine symbol, small groups emerged everywhere. Young and old were swept away by the fever of freedom. One of the tasks was to deal with the collaborators—"les collaborateurs"—among which especially loathed were the women who had been with Germans. The shaved head became their mark of shame.

bocage—the impenetrable hedgerow country that proved such a nightmare for the invaders once they moved off the beaches. Montgomery took the brunt of the criticism—from colleagues and press alike. He was too cautious, too unwilling to risk his resources, it was said.

But Monty should not be faulted—except for his overly optimistic statements and exaggerated claims. Frankly, the British soldier was not ready for the challenge. Much of the problem was a justifiable reaction to the hard experiences of D-Day. It was not cowardliness, nor incompetence—it was weariness.

On the American side the problem was much the same. In addition, the men lacked experience, having to adapt to new tactics of fighting in the bocage, a battlefield favoring the defenders.

However, it would be unfair not to note the effect the fighting capacity of the German soldier had on Allied morale. Not only better disciplined, he was also driven by a desperation derived from the perception that this was the last stand.

Perhaps one of the most profound reasons for the lack of true fighting spirit during the weeks following D-Day is to be found in the fact that the Allies enjoyed an endless supply of materiel.

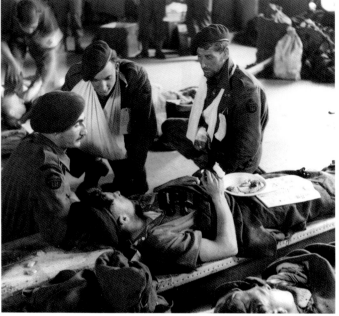

DIFFERENTLY ROLL THE DICE OF DESTINY
• •

More than fifty thousand Germans lost their lives in Normandy. The death toll among Allied soldiers was about half, but added to this should be the many thousands of airmen who died in Overlord and its aftermath. To be slightly wounded was perhaps the luckiest lot: British soldiers (left) await evacuation, and Americans (above) begin their journey back to safety. The two soldiers pictured opposite (far left), undoubtedly considered themselves lucky to have survived the inferno on the beaches, and doubly lucky to have a day of rest in the company of two helpful local girls. Not everyone made it to Berlin. For some, the end of the road was a humiliating march under enemy guard: British POWs (opposite top) captured during the fighting around Caen.

This knowledge fostered a mentality of reliance on the machine rather than on the individual initiative. It is generally accepted that when the victories in Normandy finally came, they were in most cases won on the back of attrition.

Cherbourg fell to the Americans on June 27. Bradley and his First Army were now free to turn south, joining Patton and his Third Army. But Montgomery was still stalled at Caen. Several breakout attempts failed, until on July 10 the British and the Canadians managed to capture a portion of the pivotal city. On July 25 came the breakthrough, followed by a ferocious push toward Falaise. Here, on August 22, the Allied armies finally met, closing their pincers around 60,000 Germans. For them, it meant the end of the road. For the Allies, the road lay open all the way to Paris—and ultimately to Berlin.

But it was on the beaches that the world first saw the dawn of Hitler's defeat. It was on the cold, blustery morning of June 6 that thousands of America's, Britain's and Canada's brave young men took the first step toward the liberation of a continent held captive by a tyrant, many of them paying the ultimate price. Fifty years later, their noble sacrifice is still remembered.